CW00595167

Aston Martin V8

ISBN 1 84155 618 1

Text and Photography
by
Colin Pitt

Published by
CP PRESS
PO BOX 2795
HOCKLEY, ESSEX. SS5 4BY
ENGLAND

© Colin Pitt, LLB 2005

All rights reserved. No part of this publication may be reproduced, stored in a retrieval system, nor transmitted in any form without written permission from CP Press. It is subject to the CPDA 1988. Nor may any of the covers of any of our publications be used without permission, with the sole exception of for review in national monthly motoring magazines.

First published June 2005

Acknowledgements

We wish to extend our sincere thanks to Desmond J. Smail, Richard Stewart Williams, Nicholas Mee and their companies for allowing us to photograph their truly superb collection of cars and including Aston Martin DB4 Zagatos and the Aston Martin V8 Racecar.

Other Titles
by CP Press

Chapters

Sir David Brown

David Brown expanded to building tractors with Harry Ferguson in 1934. In 1951 the David Brown Corporation was formed. David Brown Holdings also embraced David brown Gear Industries – one of the biggest manufacturers of industrial gears.

David Brown visited the Feltham factory, tried the Atom saloon and bought the company with Claude Hill and Gordon Sutherland remaining.

Alan Good of Lagonda launched the LB6 in 1945 calling it the Lagonda – Bentley. A lawsuit with Rolls followed which Lagonda lost and Alan Good put Lagonda up for sale.

David Brown learnt that Rootes and Jaguar were interested in Lagonda but were deterred by the economic outlook. David brown eventually bought the company, though not its premises, for £52,000.

Initially Aston Martin DB2/4 bodies were built by Mulliners and the Lagondas went to Tickford, Newport Pagnell. Tickford became part of the David Brown empire in 1955 and DB2/4 bodies then went there. For David Brown the best way of promoting the road cars and proving their components was to go racing. This affected much of his thinking and of those he employed.

At the same time that Aston Martin was sold to Company Developments (1972), so the tractor division was sold to Tenneco. David Brown died in 1993.

Harold Beach

Born in 1913, Harold Beach started his working life as an apprentice at the coachbuilding firm Barkers, who made Rolls-Royce bodies. After that he took a job with William Beardmore (builders of commercial vehicles) as a draughtsman at their Earlsfield factory. Then Harold Beach spent a period with another ex-Barkers employee, James Ridlington. As the war approached there was another job change for Harold Beach, this time with the Hungarian engineer Straussler at his Park Royal factory as a designer working on airfield components.

Aston Martin – The Key Players

In 1950, Harold Beach saw an advert for a design draughtsman for David Brown Tractors (Engineering) Automobile Division at Feltham. After an interview with the chief draughtsman, Frank Ayto, Harold Beach started in September 1950.

Harold Beach started work on a successor to the Aston Martin DB2 at the time Eberan von Eberhorst was made chief engineer. Von Eberhorst had been with Auto-Union before the war. But Harold Beach was to find that Eberan von Eberhorst had different ideas to him and scrapped all the work they had done on a DB2 successor.

Harold Beach was involved with work on a replacement for the Aston Martin DB2/4 and this was called Project 114. But once again his plans were to be thrown into disarray. John Wyer, who had been appointed competitions manager in 1950, was made general manager in 1956. Wyer had the idea that they should go to Touring of Milan for them to style a body on Harold Beach's perimeter frame. They turned round and said they did not want to build on Beach's design but wanted a platform frame instead. Beach's front and rear suspension of Project 114 were however retained. Harold Beach's proposed perimeter frame regarded the chassis as separate from the body, while Touring of Milan's platform frame regarded the chassis and body as almost one.

The "Superleggera" principle involves a strong platform chassis and a steel framework onto which the body panels are fixed. Components such as wheel arches are thereby part of the chassis and not added afterwards gaining greater stiffness.

Harold Beach also worked closely with Tadek Marek on the redesign of the 2.9 litre engine.

The Aston Martin DBS was introduced in 1967 and Harold Beach was responsible for its chassis and suspension. And it featured a de Dion rear axle that Harold Beach had proposed on a production model ten years earlier.

In 1972, David Brown, who had owned Aston Martin since Harold Beach joined them 22 years previously, sold the company to a property company called Company Developments. They decided to keep Harold Beach on.

In 1973 the chairman, William Willson, made Harold Beach director of engineering.

From June 1975, Harold Beach continued to work with the new owners Peter Sprague and George Minden, though no longer as a director.

Harold Beach retired in 1978, having served under three ownerships.

Aston Martin – The Key Players

Tadek Marek

Tadek Marek was born in Krakow, Poland in 1908. He graduated from Charlottenburg Technical Institute in Berlin with a diploma in engineering.

After the war Tadek and his wife Peggy went to Germany for a short period but returned again to Britain.

In 1948 he got a job with the Austin Motor Corporation at Longbridge.

He left Austin and despite a job offer with Holden Motors in Australia, went to Aston Martin. It was probably Feltham general manager James Stirling who was responsible for bringing Tadek Marek to Aston Martin.

The 1950's saw many significant Aston Martin characters coming and going. In 1950, Harold Beach, John Wyer and Robert Eberan von Eberhorst joined the development team. Others who joined included stylist Frank Feeley, chief draughtsman Frank Ayto and designer Willy Watson.

Among those who left Aston Martin were Gordon Sutherland, Jock St. John Horsfall and Claude Hill.

When Tadek Marek had finished his apprenticeship under Harold Beach he made improvements to the old 2.9 engine which was a temporary measure until the introduction of an all-new unit.

The "new" 2.9 litre engine was first seen in the DB Mark III that was introduced in March 1957 and although the cubic capacity remained the same it had a new block, new crankcase and new oil pump.

Tadek's redesign of the 2.9 engine showed his talent for this sort of work and gave Aston Martin breathing space until work could begin on an all-new engine for the all-new Aston Martin DB4.

What shortcomings that remained in Tadek Marek's 3.7 litre engine for the Aston Martin DB4 were finally put right in the 4.0 litre engine that was fitted to the Aston Martin DB5 in July 1963.

In the early 1960's John Wyer decided work should commence on a new engine to power the next generation of Aston Martins and concluded a V8 configuration would be best. Tadek began work on designing this engine in 1963. As it came from the drawing board the unit was a 4.8 litre capable of developing 324 bhp with four vertical twin choke carburettors.

Tadek Marek did all the engine design drawings himself and he had a man in the design department working for him called Alan Crouch who did all the design and layout work.

Aston Martin – The Key Players

Victor Gauntlett

Born in 1942, Victor Gauntlett made much of his money from the petrochemicals industry.

In 1980, Victor Gauntlett put £500,000 into Aston Martin Lagonda which amounted to a ten per cent stake. In 1981 he became executive chairman at a time when Aston Martin were producing four cars a week. It was Victor Gauntlett who, in the 1980's, renewed the association with Zagato and Aston Martin sold fifty-two Vantage Zagato couples which cost £86,000 each.

Prior to coming to Aston Martin he had founded and sold Pace Petroleum and in 1988 he founded Proteus Petroleum. He died in 2003, aged 60

Aston Martin – The Key Players

Alan Curtis

Alan Curtis had been interested in Aston Martin in 1975 and had been prepared to pay £650,000 for the company. But he learned it had been bought by a consortium comprising Peter Sprague (an American) and George Minden (a Canadian). But the Englishman of the consortium was no longer involved and Peter Sprague called Alan Curtis saying he had heard that he was interested in saving the company and that without an Englishman he (Peter Sprague) would not continue.

So in 1975, Aston Martin Lagonda's quartet of shareholders were Peter Sprague, George Minden, Alan Curtis and a retired steel businessman Denis Flather.

At the end of 1975, Alan Curtis along with Denis Flather became directors of Aston Martin. In March 1977, Alan Curtis became managing director of Aston Martin.

Four members of the senior management were made associate directors and these were Mike Loasby (director of engineering), David Flink (director of manufacturing), Nigel Butten (director of finance) and Tony Nugent (director of sales).

Rex Woodgate

Rex Woodgate was born in 1926 and had a job as an equipment tester at British Acoustic Films. Then he got a job with Thomson and Taylor who built racing and record breaking cars at Brooklands. He worked as a mechanic to Stirling Moss, preparing his car for the 1949 season, before joining H.W. Motors of Walton-on-Thames as a mechanic until 1950. Reg Parnell recommended Rex Woodgate to John Wyer and he was engaged to build production versions of the Aston Martin DB3S in 1954.

Rex Woodgate also worked on the DB3S's replacement the DBR1 and then the DBR2.

In the middle of 1961, Rex Woodgate rejoined Aston Martin and was factory service representative for North America. Rex Woodgate was convinced that Aston Martin should set up its own importership rather than using several importers and distributors. In May 1964, Aston Martin Lagonda Incorporated was opened near Philadelphia and it stayed there for fourteen years.

In 1971, Rex Woodgate was made President of Aston Martin Lagonda Incorporated.

John Wyer

John Wyer was made Competitions Manager at Aston Martin in 1950 and was made General manager in 1956. Reg Parnell succeeded him as Competitions Manager.

John Wyer had been pit manager of Dudley Folland's privately entered pre-war Aston Martin. Upon retirement he went to live in Arizona and he died in 1989.

Aston Martin – The Key Players

William Towns

In 1936 William Towns was born, fairly near to Guildford. In 1955 William Towns joined the Rootes Company and found that there was a department within the Rootes Company that did in full size what he had done as a lad with plasticine. The person in charge of Rootes' styling studio at the time was Ted White. Ted White as the department Head of Styling was more an administrator than stylist because management (seven members of the Rootes family) were the stylists and the supposed stylists were more akin to modellors for the management.

William Towns stayed with Rootes for eight years before moving to Rover for more money and at a time the Rover 2000 was being developed. William Lyons, upon seeing the full-scale wooden mock-up of the Rover 2000, thought that its styling was abysmal and that it was badly proportioned. But Towns thought that the interior was excellent.

While at Rover, William Towns worked on three projects. The first involved working on proposals for a Targa-topped two plus two sports car based on the Rover 2000 saloon. Sketches were made but nothing came of them. William Towns next project concerned the gas turbine racer that was developed for Le Mans. For the 1963 Le Mans the gas turbine racer was entered as an open roadster. But for the 1965 Le Mans, William Towns was to develop a closed body vbersion of the gas turbine racer. Towns produced a scale model which was subsequently wind tunnel tested before being made into a full-size body. The third project was a car intended for the film world. William Towns drew up a very low sports, based again on the Rover 2000 platform. Although a quarter-scale model was made nothing came of it once again.

William Towns had been at Rover three years when somebody mentioned that there was a job going at Aston Martin. But Aston Martin did not have a styling job on offer, they had openings for a body engineer and for a seat designer. William Towns went to them and they offered him a job designing seats at first.

Later, Harold Beach told William Towns they wanted to do a four door car. Towns explained that you have to design the four door version first and then shorten it if you wish to make a two door. William Towns was later asked to produce scale models of his proposals and he created a two door and a four door side by side. The latter became the Lagonda model of 1974.

In 1969 William Towns was offered the job of Chief Stylist at Triumph but he preferred to work for them on a freelance basis. Replacements for the

Triumph 1300 and 2000 saloons (code-named Puma and Bobcat) were cars that Towns was brought in to work on.

Aston Martin kept in touch with William Towns and when the 6-cylinder Aston Martin DBS became the V8 he produced the styling. However, proposals for gull-winged versions of an Aston Martin and Lagonda came to nothing.

Aston Martin – The Key Players

Augustus Bertelli

Many regard Augustus Bertelli as the father of Aston Martin. Bertelli was born in the Italian town of Genoa in 1890; he and his family moved to Cardiff in 1894. On leaving school he took up a general engineering apprenticeship in Cardiff. He then, took a job with Fiat in Turin. Bertelli was riding mechanic to Felice Nazzaro in a Fiat for the Coppa Florio. Grahame-Whites, manufacturers of French aircraft, took Bertelli on to develop an engine of his.

Augustus Cesare Bertelli married Vera in 1918 at Hendon, and they moved to Golders Green. Bertelli was given a job at Birmingham-based Alldays and Onions and he designed a new Enfield-Alldays car.

In 1924, Bertelli and W.S. Renwick teamed up in business in Birmingham. Renwick and Bertelli bought Aston Martin from John Benson and kept him on. Really, John Benson had nothing but the goodwill of Aston Martin. Augustus Bertelli and W.S. Renwick then moved to Feltham and they then took on Claude Hill. Within a year of starting at Feltham, they had produced a completely new Aston Martin with a 1 ½ litre engine. The end of the 1920s and the start of the 1930s saw the Aston Martin name carried on the 1 ½ litre series and had names such as International, Ulster and Le Mans.

Augustus Bertelli's brother, Enrico Bertelli, ran a coach-building business next to the Aston Martin factory at Feltham, hence the beautiful bodies of the early Aston Martin cars in an era of genuine hand-built cars.

Benson and Renwick eventually left the company and Claude Hill left twice, once in 1928 and once in 1934. In 1936, Bertelli left and the company was in the control of the Sutherland family at a time when the 2-litre cars were being introduced.

Just before World War II, Bertelli took a job with a firm called High Duty Alloys, where he stayed until 1955.

Aston Martin – Prototypes

Aston Martin prototype the R110 (front view)

Aston Martin prototype the R110 (side view)

Aston Martin Lagonda 3 and 4 Litre Cars

In 1957 the last of the 3 litre Lagondas were made. David Brown wanted its replacement to be based on a lengthened Aston Martin DB4 engine extended to 4 litres.

The Lagonda Rapide was not announced in 1961 and only 55 were sold from 1961 to 1964. The car used a 4 litre version of the Aston Martin DB4 engine which had a 4mm overbore. It also featured a De Dion rear axle.

Lagonda Rapide – On its 4 litre engine the bore was 4mm larger than its 92mm stroke

Aston Martin Lagonda 3 and 4 Litre Cars

Sir David Brown's 1969 Lagonda saw production in October 1974. It had four doors and a grill that did not look like an Aston Martin grill.

Priced at £14,040 in the UK only 4 were built by the end of 1974.

Aston Martin Lagonda

The Aston Martin Lagonda project started in January 1976, with the first example appearing at the October 1976 London Motor Show. The super styling came from William Towns, who had worked for Aston Martin since 1976.

Each car cost £74,004. William Towns designed the shape so it could be produced in either two door or four door form which is why there is a glass panel in the roof.

Initially the Aston Martin Lagonda driver was faced by a vacuum fluorescent liquid crystal instrument display. Aston Martin were one of the first manufacturers to offer such a technologically advanced system. The instrumentation was unique at the time and led to the car being called the "world's fastest calculator". As other cars began to appear with similar LCD instrumentation, Aston Martin decided to go one better and have aircraft instrument manufacturer Javelina of Dallas develop a cathode ray tube instrument display. In essence there are three mini TV screens set in the dashboard. This desire for technology backfired on one occasion. It was the occasion of the first car (chassis 13008) being handed over to Lady Tavistock in April 1978. The Aston Martin Lagonda had to be pushed to the ceremony, in view of the press, as the Cranfield Institute of Technology were still working on the car's computer. It had been too late to install it! The engine of the Aston Martin Lagonda is the same 5340cc V8 that is fitted to all the Aston Martins. This engine has a twin overhead cam per bank arrangement atop hemispherically shaped combustion chambers. Four twin choke Weber aspirated units move the car from nought to sixty in 8.8 seconds.

Drive is taken to the rear wheels by a Chrysler Torqueflite three-speed automatic gearbox.

Aston Martin Lagonda

Aston Martin Lagonda

DP2034 Prototype

Although Aston Martin Lagondas were four door cars, as the above photograph shows, chassis number DP2034 (Prototype) was the one and only two-door Lagonda Coupe. Wheel arches on the DP2034 Prototype were flared to accommodate sixteen-inch wheels. The purpose of the 300mm shortened Lagonda was to develop the Aston Martin Virage chassis. The car was completed in October 1986. It was fitted with an Aston Martin European EFI two-valve engine and five-speed manual ZF gearbox.

Aston Martin Lagonda

Triple front light assembly of the Lagonda

Rear of the Lagonda shows the Aston Martin badge

Aston Martin Lagonda

This Aston Martin Lagonda is registered F 488 DEX

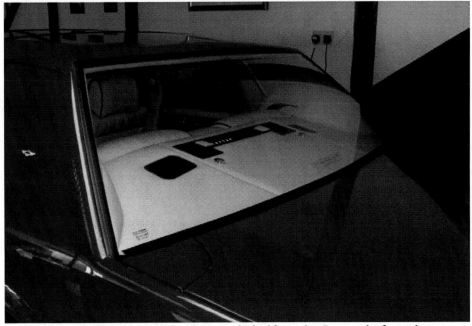

Rear windscreen and back parcel shelf on the Lagonda four-door

Aston Martin – V8 Engine

Tadek Marek entrusted a block re-design to Alan Crouch who strengthened the block with extra ribs, thicker mounting flanges and wider bearing caps. Cylinder head studs were extended down to the base of the block. But the problem for Aston Martin was that the V8 engine, even at 5 litres, was barely faster than the old straight-six Aston Martin DB6. So the bore was increased again to 100 millimetres and the stroke was increased to 85 millimetres to give 5340cc.

The block is a sandcasting in LM8 aluminium alloy. It has chrome-vanadium iron wet liners which protrude above the block face by 0.004 inches. There are three grooves in each wet liner's base. The upper and lower grooves house O-rings. The middle grooves line up with a hole in the block. The block extends down past the crankshaft centre line to provide walls for the main-bearing buttresses. A cast aluminium sump seals the engines underside.

The crankshaft is a hollow forging of EN 19T chrome molybdenum steel. It features large plugs in the webs next to the crankpins. A small duplex chain drives an eccentric-lobe oil pump from the nose of the crankshaft. A larger duplex chain drives an intermediate sprocket mounted in line with (but not attached to) the water pump.

Cam timing adjustment is by tightening clamp nuts on the slotted timing sprockets.

Aston Martin – V8 Engine

From 1973 the Aston Martin V8 engine reverted to four carburettors. The regular Aston Martin V8 engine continued in V8s and Lagondas until Weber-Marelli fuel injection took over.

Vantage version engines with new camshafts, bigger valves and four 48 IDF carburettors (with a 32% power increase) were available up until 1989.

At the end of 1968 it was decided that the capacity of the engine would be increased to 5340cc by increasing the bore to 100 millimetres and the stroke to 85 millimetres.

Aston Martin – V8 Engine

In March 1969 the first of the 5340cc engines (V535/001/PX) went to Bosch complete with cast inlet manifolds, air filters. They had a 9 to 1 compression ratio with 343bhp at 5500rpm.

A second unit with downdraught Webers produced 365bhp at 6000rpm, and had a 9.5 to 1 compression ratio.

A third engine with carburettors gave 384bhp at 5800rpm.

In October 1969 the V/540 series engine gave 310bhp-320bhp at 5000rpm.

Aston Martin – V8 Engine

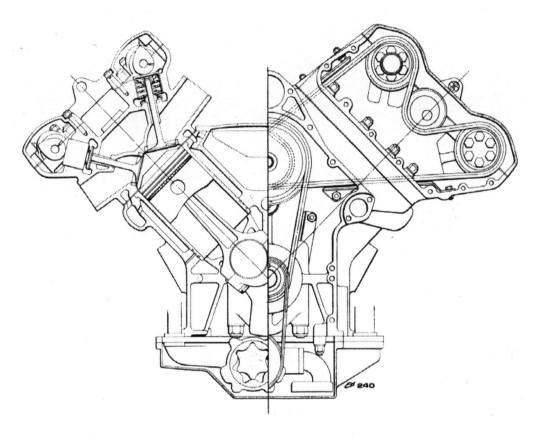

Two level section of the 5 litre V8 Aston Martin racing engine

Aston Martin – V8 Engine

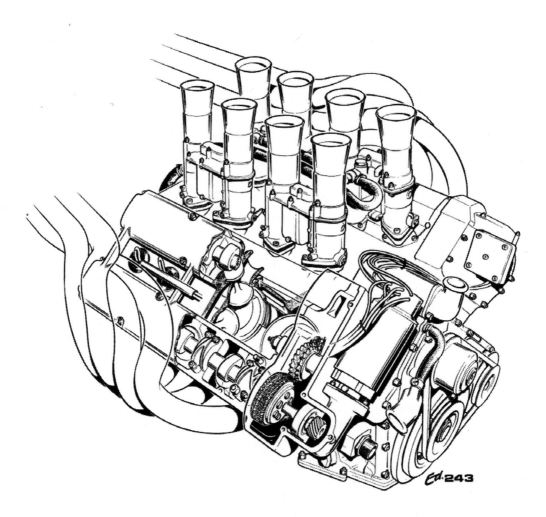

Cutaway view of the 5 litre Aston Martin racing engine

Aston Martin – V8 Engine

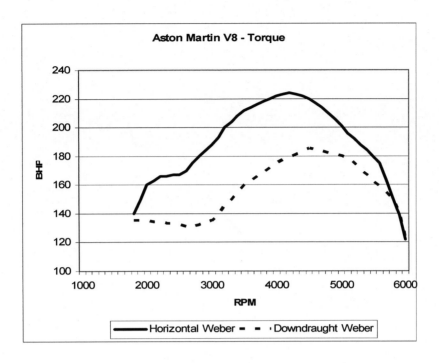

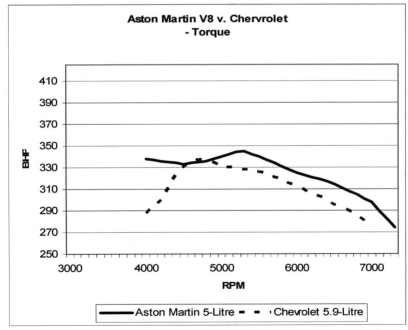

Aston Martin – V8 Engine

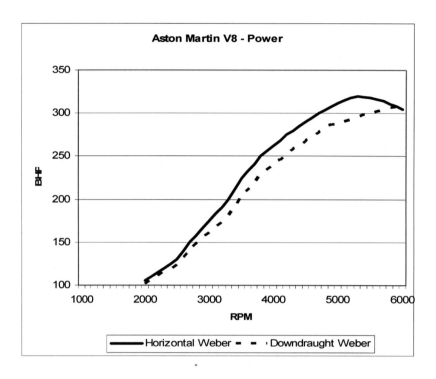

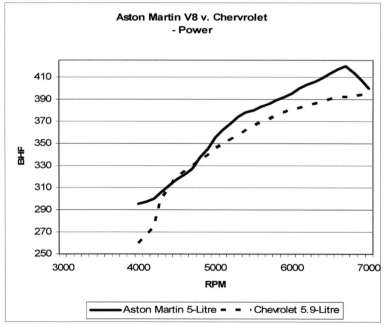

Aston Martin Project 212, 214, 215 Cars

Project 212, above, before Le Mans 1962

The car was exceptionally fast but was not that stable at high speeds. DP212, later referred to as MP212, went to Silverstone in September of 1962. It should have been successful in the hands of Graham Hill and Richie Ginther but it retired on lap 79 of the 1962 Le Mans race.

Aston Martin DP214, DP215 Project Cars

The 1963 cars for endurance racing were more serious contenders than Project 212, and were two Project 214 cars and a Project 215 car.

The Project 214, or MP214, cars used Aston Martin DB4 GT chassis numbers, 0194/R and 0195/R. The MP214s used 3.7 litre engines, whilst the MP215 used a 3995cc engine. MP215 had an even lighter boxed girder. It also had independent rear suspension and the five-speed transaxle from the Aston Martin DBR1. It featured a cut-off Kamm tail.

The interior of Project 215, which bears the registration plate XMO 88.

Aston Martin DP214, DP215 Project Cars

The interior of the racing Project 215 car

Another interior view of the Project 215 car

Aston Martin DP214, DP215
Racing Record

Date	Race	Drivers	Position
15-16 Jun 63	Le Mans 24 Hours (Aston Martin DP214 Car Number 7 Chassis Number 0194/R Completed 139 laps in Grand Touring Group)	William Kimberly/ Jo Schlesser	Did not finish
15-16 Jun 63	Le Mans 24 Hours (Aston Martin DP215 Car Number 18 Completed 29 laps in Prototype GT Group)	Phil Hill/ Lucien Bianchi	Did not finish
23 Aug 63	Tourist Trophy (GB) (Aston Martin DP214 Car Number 2 Chassis Number 0194/R Completed 128 laps in GT Division 3 Group)	Innes Ireland/ William Kimberly	7th place
23 Aug 63	Tourist Trophy (GB) (Aston Martin DP214 Car Number 1 Chassis Number 0195/R Completed 94 laps in GT Division 3 Group)	Bruce McLaren/ William Kimberley	Did not finish
Scrutineers decided the wheel rims did not conform to the homologation papers, so the cars ran on reduced track.			
8 Sep 63	Monza Coppa Inter-Europa (Aston Martin DP214 Car Number 46 Chassis Number 0194/R Completed 101 laps)	Roy Salvadori	1st place
Salvadori beat Mike Parkes in a Ferrari 250 GTO.			
8 Sep 63	Monza Coppa Inter-Europa (Aston Martin DP214 Car Number 45 Chassis Number 0195/R Completed 98 laps)	Lucien Bianchi	3rd place

Aston Martin DP214, DP215
Racing Record

Date	Race	Drivers	Position
16 Feb 64	Daytona 2000km (Aston Martin DP214 Car Number 27 Chassis Number 0195/R Completed 243 laps)	Brian Hetreed/ Chris Kerrison	Not running at finish
16 Feb 64	Daytona 2000km (Aston Martin DP214 Car Number 26 Chassis Number 0194/R Completed 34 laps)	Roy Salvadori/ Mike Salmon	Did not finish
17 May 64	Spa-Francorchamps 500km (Aston Martin DP214 Car Number 7 Chassis Number 0195/R)	Brian Hetreed	Did not finish
17 May 64	Spa-Francorchamps 500km (Aston Martin DP214 Car Number 6 Chassis Number 0194/R)	Mike Salmon	Did not finish
21-22 Jun 64	Le Mans 24 Hours (Aston Martin DP214 Car Number 18 Chassis Number 0194/R Completed 235 laps)	Mike Salmon/ Peter Sutcliffe	Did not finish
29 Aug 64	Tourist Trophy (GB) (Aston Martin DP214 Car Number 34 Chassis Number 0194/R Completed 108 laps)	Mike Salmon	13th place

When John Wyer left to join the Ford GT40 programme this marked the end of Aston Martin in racing with the Project cars. MP212 and two 214s were acquired by Dawnay racing.

Aston Martin DBS
October 1967 to May 1972

William Towns, who had joined Aston Martin as a seat designer, made a name for himself when he designed the Aston Martin DBS. The design he had done as a clay model went into production virtually unaltered. The Aston Martin DBS was about a couple of inches shorter than its DB6 predecessor, achieved mainly by reducing rear overhang. However the Aston Martin DBS was four and a half inches wider than its DB6 predecessor. However with wider wheels and the necessary clearance the Aston Martin DBS emerged as a car having a width of six feet. That is six inches more than its predecessor the Aston Martin DB6

A side profile of the Aston Martin DBS

Aston Martin DBS
October 1967 to May 1972

The overall height of the Aston Martin DBS was four feet four inches but the roof line fell away quicker than the roof line of the Aston Martin DB6. Front seats were lowered by about an inch and rear seats were lowered by about two and a half inches.

Aston Martin cross members had to be beefed up to keep a torsionally stiff chassis. Consequently, the chassis of the DBS was so substantially changed that new jigs were required rather than being able to use modified Aston Martin DB6 jigs.

Despite all the work involved with creating a new shape for the Aston Martin DBS, the first prototype was finished on 17th July 1967. It underwent wind-tunnel and track testing the following day.

Rear side view of GKX 8G

Aston Martin DBS
October 1967 to May 1972

Weight distribution of the Aston Martin DBS was shown to be 48 / 52 as against 49 ¼ / 50 ¾ for the Aston Martin DB6.

Early Aston Martin DBS cars had a single control for heating but the heating system was not the car's strongest point. One feature of the Aston Martin DBS that disappeared five years into production was the five and three-quarter inch headlights fitted four-up in an Aston Martin shaped grille. The design reverted to seven inch lights fitted two-up in an Aston Martin grille. This had been considered, though not adopted, at the original design stage.

Halfway through 1968, Aston Martin DB6s and Aston Martin DBSs were being produced in equal numbers (the DBS did not replace the DB6 straight away). About five Aston Martin DBSs and five Aston Martin DB6s were being produced each week.

Aston Martin DBS
October 1967 to May 1972
Production Figures

Aston Martin DBS	829 cars
Chassis numbers ran from	DBS 5001/R to DBS 5829/R
Aston Martin AM Vantage	71 cars
Chassis numbers ran from	AM/6001/R to AM/6070/R

Development of the bodyline on the Aston Martin DBS eliminated the need for an up-lipped spoiler

Aston Martin DBS
October 1967 to May 1972

A side view of the Aston Martin DBS

The car was 15 feet 1 ¼ inches long, 6 feet wide, had a height of 4 feet 4 inches and weighed 31 ¼ cwt. Its top speed was 142 mph.

Aston Martin DBS
October 1967 to May 1972

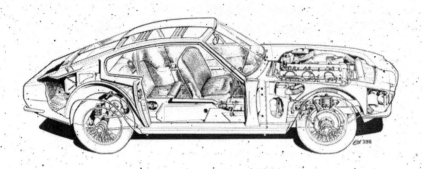

Cutaway drawing of the Aston Martin DBS

A rear view of the Aston Martin DBS

Aston Martin DBS
Technical Specifications

ENGINE

Cylinders	6, in line
Main Bearings	7
Cooling System	Water; pump, viscous fan and thermostat
Bore	96mm (3.78in)
Stroke	92mm (3.62in)
Displacement	3,995cc (244 cu. in.)
Valve Gear	Twin overhead camshafts
Compression Ratio	9.4 to 1; Min. Octane rating: 100 RM
Carburettors	3 twin-choke Weber 45 DCOE
Fuel Pump	Twin, SU electric
Oil Filter	Full flow, renewable element
Max. Power	325 bhp (net) at 5,750 rpm
Max. Torque	290 lb. ft. (net) at 4,500 rpm

TRANSMISSION

Clutch	Borg and Beck, diaphragm, 9.25 in. dia.
Gearbox	ZF, five-speed, all synchromesh
Gear Ratios	Top 0.834
	Fourth 1.00
	Third 1.23
	Second 1.76
	First 2.73
	Reverse 3.31
Final Drive	Hypoid bevel, 3.73 to 1, limited slip

CHASSIS and BODY

Construction	Steel platform chassis and light alloy body

SUSPENSION

Front	Independent, wishbones, coil springs, anti-roll bar, telescopic dampers
Rear	De Dion axle, coil springs, trailing arms, Watts linkage, Armstrong Selectaride lever arm dampers

Aston Martin DBS
Technical Specifications

STEERING

Make and Type	Rack and Pinion
Wheel diameter	16 in.

BRAKES

Make and Type	Girling, disc front and rear
Servo	Twin vacuum
Dimensions	F. 11.5 in. dia..; R. 10.8 in. dia.
Swept Area	F. 241 sq. in.; R. 197 sq. in. Total 438 sq. in. (237 sq. in. ton laden)

WHEELS

Type	Centre lock, wire spokes, 6 in. wide rim
Tyres – make	Avon
Tyres – type	Radial-ply, tubed
Tyres – size	205 VR-15 in.

EQUIPMENT

Battery	12-volt, 60-Ah
Alternator	Lucas, 11-amp a.c.
Headlamps	Lucas, four quartz-iodine lamp system, 220/110-watt (total)
Reversing Lamp	Twin standard
Electric Fuses	12
Screen Wipers	2-speed, self-parking
Screen Washer	Standard, electric pump
Interior Heater	Standard, air-blending
Heated Backlight	Standard
Safety Belts	Standard
Interior Trim	Leather seats, pvc headlining
Floor Covering	Carpet
Starting Handle	No provision
Jack	Hydraulic pillar
Jacking Points	4, under chassis
Windscreen	Laminated
Underbody Protection	Rubberized undersealing on surfaces exposed to road

Aston Martin DBS
Technical Specifications

MAINTENANCE

Fuel Tank	21 Imp. Gallons (3 gal. reserve) (95.5 litres)
Cooling System	28 pints (including heater)
Engine Sump	24 pints (13.6 litres) SAE 10W/40. Change oil every 2,500 miles. Change filter element every 5,000 miles.
Gearbox	3.5 pints SAE 90. Change oil every 10,000 miles.
Final Drive	3.25 pints SAE 90. Change oil every 10,000 miles.
Grease	11 points every 2,500 miles
Tyre Pressures	F. 30; R. 30 psi (normal driving)
	F. 35, R. 35 psi (fast driving over 115 mph)

PERFORMANCE DATA

5th Gear mph per 1,000 rpm	26.1
Mean Piston Speed at Max. Power	3,470 ft/min
Bhp per ton laden	176.2

Speed Range, Gear Ratios and Time in Seconds

Mph	5th (3.11)	4th (3.73)	3rd (4.60)	2nd (6.58)	1st (10.1)
10-30				4.9	2.8
20-40			7.1	3.9	2.4
30-50		8.2	5.9	3.7	
40-60	11.4	8.0	5.9	3.9	
50-70	10.6	7.6	6.0	3.9	
60-80	10.2	7.1	5.1		
70-90	10.7	7.1	5.4		
80-100	11.0	7.5	6.7		
90-110	11.6	8.2			
100-120	16.0	10.4			

Aston Martin DBS
Technical Specifications

Maximum Speeds

Gear	mph	kph	rpm
Top (mean)	140	226	5,350
Top (best)	143	230	5,500
4th	125	201	5,750
3rd	101	163	5,750
2nd	71	114	5,750
1st	46	74	5,750

Fuel(constant speed-mpg-5th)

30 mph	19.8
40 mph	18.6
50 mph	18.4
60 mph	18.7
70 mph	18.4
80 mph	15.7
90 mph	14.5
100 mph	13.0

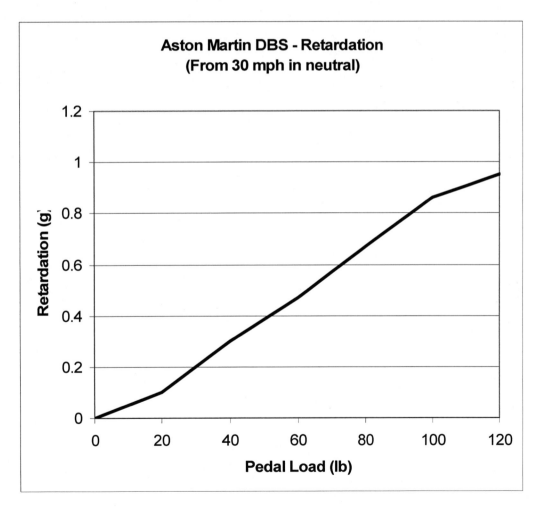

**Aston Martin DBS - Retardation
(From 30 mph in neutral)**

Aston Martin DBS
Technical Specifications

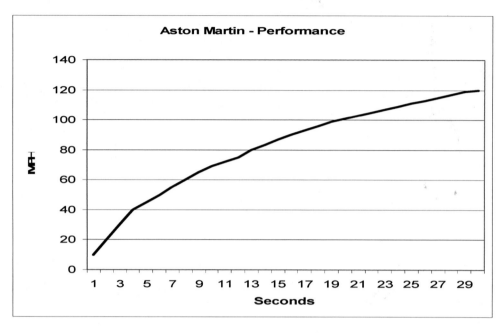

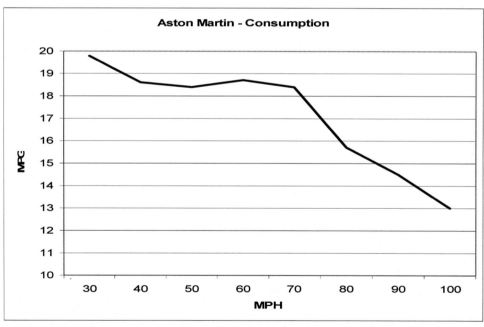

Aston Martin DBS, DBSV8 and Vantage
Specifications, Dimensions and Performance

Specifications	DBS	DBSV8	Vantage
Engine	In-line six	90 degree V8	90 degree V8
Bore/stroke	96x92mm	100x85mm	100x85mm
Capacity	3995cc	5340cc	5340cc
Valves	dohc	dohc per bank	dohc per bank
Compression	8.9:1	9.0:1	9.0:1
Power	282bhp (NET) @ 5500rpm	Not quoted	Not quoted
Torque	280lbs ft (NET) @ 4500rpm	Not quoted	Not quoted
Transmission	5 speed manual or 3 speed automatic	5 speed manual or 3 speed automatic	5 speed manual
Final Drive	3.73:1 manual, 3.54:1 automatic	3.54:1 manual, 3.31:1 automatic	3.45:1
Suspension (front)	Ind by wishbones, coil springs, dampers, anti-roll bar	Ind by wishbones, coil springs, dampers, anti-roll bar	Ind by wishbones, coil springs, dampers, anti-roll bar
Suspension (rear)	De Dion tube, trailing links, Watts linkage, Selectaride Dampers	De Dion tube, trailing links, Watts linkage, telescopic dampers	De Dion tube, trailing links, Watts linkage. telescopic dampers
Steering	Rack and pinion, power assisted	Rack and pinion, power assisted	Rack and pinion, power assisted
Brakes	Discs all round	Discs all round	Discs all round

Aston Martin DBS, DBSV8 and Vantage
Specifications, Dimensions and Performance

Dimensions	DBS	DBSV8	Vantage
Length	15ft 0.5in	15ft 0.5in	15ft 3.75in
Width	6ft 0in	6ft 0in	6ft 0in
Height	4ft 5in	4ft 5in	4ft 5in
Wheelbase	8ft 6.7in	8ft 6.7in	8ft 6.7in
Weight	3500lbs	3584lbs	3808lbs

Performance	DBS	DBSV8	Vantage
Max speed	140mph	161mph	168mph
0-60mph	8.6secs	6.0secs	5.4secs
0-100mph	19.6secs	14.7secs	13.0secs
Standing ¼ mile	16.3secs	14.3secs	13.7secs

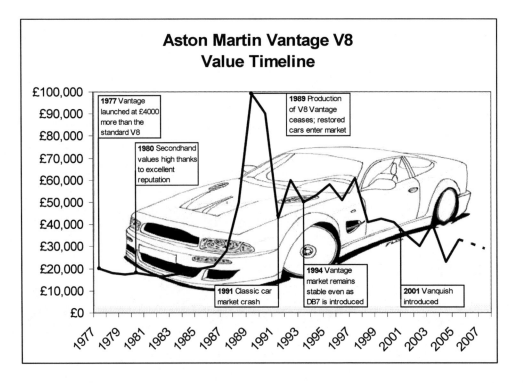

44

Aston Martin V8 – RHAM-001
(Robin Hamilton Aston Martin V8)

Robin Hamilton was an Aston Martin dealer based at Fauld near Tutbury on the outskirts of Burton on Trent. In 1972 when they moved to nearby Fauld, he was joined by Mervyn Sheppard, who was chief engineer.

He dreamt of taking Aston Martin back to Le Mans and being a former Rolls Royce apprentice and amateur racer, was able to convert a V8 into something more akin to a racing GT car.

Aston Martin as a company did not wish to be involved but were prepared to help where they could. Mike Loasby helped with the car and its engine development. Robin Hamilton's engine developed 480 bhp with its Weber IDA carburettors.

RHAM-001 weighed 1516kg on the scales. It started life as DBSV8/10038/RC and when it appeared in April 1976 at Silverstone the car looked nothing like its appearance above, where it had been converted to Le Mans specifications.

Aston Martin V8 – RHAM-001
(Robin Hamilton Aston Martin V8)

When Rolls Royce's Aero division faced closure in 1971, Robin Hamilton became an Aston Martin Specialist and campaigned a DB4 GT as a way of promoting the business. In 1972, Robin Hamilton Motors gained factory status as a service agent and he next turned his eye to campaigning an Aston Martin V8.

At its Silverstone debut in May 1977, in Group 5 category the car was up against Turbo Porsches. It circulated in the top 10 but heat soak from the inboard rear disc brakes caused problems. Repairs were made and the car finished but it was too far behind to be officially placed.

Having been given Nimonic steel valves, forged Cosworth pistons and a redesigned sump and being capable of 400 lb/feet of torque at 5,250 rpm on Weber 50 IDA downdraught carburettors, the car had to run in Group 5 and not Group 4.

Chassis number 10038/RC or RHAM-001 as it became known

Aston Martin V8 – RHAM-001
(Robin Hamilton Aston Martin V8)

Wind-tunnel testing of the car, paid for by Aston Martin, had indicated the car was likely to have dangerously high lift at speed; a spoiler was the answer. Fitment of a rear spoiler on just one car necessitated the move from Group 4 to Group 5 however. Wind-tunnel testing had also indicated that a reduction of front area weight (by putting the radiator at the back) would be beneficial. But in testing like this the car ran too hot and the radiator was returned to the front. Four engine oil coolers were used on the car.

After the Le Mans event of 1977, Robin Hamilton was convinced that if the Aston Martin V8 – RHAM – 001 had had a larger fuel tank – allowed in the GTP class – and therefore had needed less fuel stops, the car would not have had brake problems and would have finished in the top ten.

For the 1978 Le Mans, Robin Hamilton had worked on a twin-turbo charged version of the V8 but with fuel consumption down to 2 ½ miles per gallon at times, he had to withdraw from the 1978 Le Mans with two weeks to go to the event.

From 1978 on, the task of obtaining sponsorship was less difficult for Robin Hamilton; Aston Martin Owner's Club member and Lola-Aston Martin owner Peter Millward providing sponsorship. Sponsorship was provided through Millward's Link Systems, a specialist manufacturer of materials analysing systems.

By the time of RHAM 001s appearance at the Silverstone 6 Hours in May 1979, the car had again changed considerably and had been streamlined and modified. By now, also, the roll cage was part of the chassis rather than being bolted to it. A larger front air dam was fitted and there were larger air ducts to the brakes. By using fuel injection instead of carburettors, fuel consumption was improved from 2 ½ mpg to 4 mpg. It could produce over 700 bhp.

The cars last publicity outing was on 14th October 1980 when RHAM 001 broke the World Land Speed record for towing a caravan at 124.91 miles per hour.

Aston Martin DBSV8/10038/RC (RHAM 001) was put up for sale in 1984 when Robin Hamilton closed his business and was bought by Chris Crawford. In 2005, the car was for sale by Nicholas Mee's Aston Martin Car Company.

A second DBS V8, a sort of quasi-Le Mans car was built by Robin Hamilton for Peter Griggs. The car was chassis number DBSV8/10071/R. The cars fuel-injected engine was prepared by Piper.

Aston Martin V8 – RHAM-001
Racing Record

17th May 1977 – Silverstone 6 Hours (GB)

Robin Hamilton and David Preece in the Aston Martin V8 (Car Number 22) were not classified after 115 laps. (RHAM 001)

11th June 1977 – Le Mans 24 Hours

Robin Hamilton, David Preece and Mike Salmon finished 17th place in the Le Mans GTP in car number 83 completing 261 laps (RHAM 001). Failed to classify as they were part of the prototype category and did not cover the required distance. The fastest lap time with Hamilton at the wheel had been 4 minutes 34.2 seconds. The car could produce 520 bhp.

Aston Martin AMV8 (RHAM/001) was also entered for the 1978 Le Mans of 10th-11th June to be driven by David Preece and Robin Hamilton but did not arrive. Lack of sponsorship probably prevented a 1978 return to Le Mans.

6th May 1979 – Silverstone 6 Hours (GB)

Robin Hamilton, Derek Bell and David Preece finished in 13th place in Group 5 after 185 laps. RHAM/001 ran as car number 12. It was entered by Robin Hamilton. Car was suffering brake problems after two and a half hours and they retired. By now the cars roofline had been lowered by three inches.

9th-10th June 1979 – Le Mans 24 Hours

The car again of Robin Hamilton, Mike Salmon and David Preece ran as car number 50 in the Le Mans GTP. Completed only 21 laps due to an oil system problem and did not finish. The car retired just two hours and forty-five minutes into the race. The car could now produce 800 bhp.

Aston Martin V8 – RHAM-001
Racing Record

11th May 1980 – Silverstone 6 Hours

The car of Robin Hamilton, Derek Bell and Willie Green ran as car number 10 in the Le Mans GTP and was entered by Simon Phillips. It did not finish and completed 20 laps. By now the car featured a rear wing to counter-balance the downforce at the front. The car retired after just 61 ½ miles with rear-hub failure.

RHAM-001 fuel cap

Aston Martin V8 – RHAM-001
Picture Gallery

Side view of RHAM-001. Nicknamed "The Muncher" as the car was heavy on brake discs

800 bhp was available from this Aston Martin V8 racer
Peter Millward's Link Systems provided sponsorship for the 1979 season.

Aston Martin V8 – RHAM-001
Picture Gallery

Cabin features red dynotape

SAS, a manufacturer of riot gear, were prepared to sponsor RHAM-001 for the
1977 Le Mans

Aston Martin DBS 6 Cylinder
Twin Test

	Aston Martin DBS 6-Cylinder	BMW 3.0 CSL 6-Cylinder
Bore and Stroke:	96.0mm x 92.0 mm	89.25 mm x 80.00 mm
Capacity:	3995 cc	3003 cc
Compression Ratio:	9.4 : 1	9.5 : 1
Power:	325 bhp @ 5750 rpm	200 bhp @ 5500 rpm
Transmission:	5-speed	4-speed
Length:	15 ft 0.5 inches	15 ft 3.4 inches
Width:	6 ft 0 inches	5 ft 6 inches
Height:	4 ft 5 inches	4 ft 5.5 inches
Wheelbase:	8 ft 6.7 inches	8 ft 7.3 inches
Maximum Speed:	140 mph	133 mph
0-60 mph:	8.6 seconds	7.3 seconds
Production Years:	1967 to 1973	1972
Numbers Built:	829	1096

The 6-cylinder Aston Martin had a turning circle diameter of 36 feet.

Aston Martin DBS V8 Saloon

Dimensions

Overall Length:	15ft 0.5 inches	(4585 mm)
Overall Width:	72 inches	(1829 mm)
Overall Height:	52 ¼ inches	(1327 mm)
Ground Clearance:	5 ½ inches	(140 mm)
Front and Rear Track: 59 inches	(1499 mm)	
Turning Circle Diameter:	38 feet	
Wheelbase:	102 ¾ inches	(2610 mm)

Suspension

Front Suspension:	Co-axial Coil Springs and shock absorbers, anti-roll bar
Number of Coils:	11 ¾
Coil Diameter:	3.7 inches
Wire Diameter:	0.515 inches
Spring Length Free:	16 inches
Spring Length Fitted:	9.66 inches
Spring Rate:	196 lb/inch
Rear Suspension:	Coil springs, parallel trailing links, WATT linkage
Number of Coils:	9
Coil Diameter:	4.5 inches
Wire Diameter:	0.5 inches
Spring Length Free:	15.25 inches
Spring Length Fitted:	9.5 inches
Spring Rate:	142 lb/inch

Aston Martin DBS V8 Saloon

Transmission

Type:	Rear Wheel Drive
Clutch:	Borg and Beck
Manual Gearbox Ratios:	0.845:1
1:1	
	1.22:1
	1.78:1
	2.90:1
	Rev 2.63:1

Automatic Gearbox Ratios:	Top 1:1
	Inter 1.45:1
	Low 2.45:1
	Rev 2.20:1

Final Drive Gear:	Hypoid, Limited-slip Differential

Final Drive Ratio:	Manual	3.54:1
	Auto	3.31:1

Diff. Bearing Pre-Load:	0.005 inches

Aston Martin DBS V8 Saloon

Engine Technical Information

Engine Type:	V8 Four-Stroke, Fuel Injection
Firing Order:	1RF – 5LF – 4 – 2 – 6 – 3 – 7 – 8
Bore and Stroke:	100 mm x 85 mm
Cubic Capacity:	5340 cc
Compression Ratio:	9.0 : 1
Piston Rings:	2 Compression, 1 Oil
Compression Piston	
Ring Width:	1.96 mm
Oil Piston	
Ring Width:	4.80 mm
Compression Piston	
Rings Groove Clearance:	0.0016 inches to 0.0032 inches
Crankpin Diameter:	2.2490 inches to 2.2485 inches
Connecting Rod Length:	6.125 inches
Big-End	
Bearing Clearance:	0.0025 inches to 0.0035 inches
Big-End	
Side Clearance:	0.0023 inches to 0.0085 inches
Main Bearing Clearance:	0.0013 inches to 0.0018 inches
Crankshaft End-Float:	0.004 inches to 0.008 inches
Crankshaft End-Thrust On:	No. 3 Main Bearing
Camshaft Bearings:	5
Camshaft	
Bearing Clearance:	0.001 inches to 0.002 inches
Camshaft End Float:	0.002 inches to 0.004 inches
Camshaft Drive Type:	Duplex Roller Chain;
	0.250 inches to 0.375 inches

Aston Martin DBS V8 Saloon

Valve Technical Information

Inlet Valve
  Head Diameter: 1.940 inches to 1.945 inches
Exhaust Valve
  Head Diameter: 1.875 inches to 1.880 inches
Inlet Valve
  Stem Diameter: 0.3419 inches to 0.3422 inches
Exhaust Valve
  Stem Diameter: 0.3414 inches to 0.3417 inches
Valve Seat Angle: 45 degrees
Inlet Valve Lift: 0.425 inches
Exhaust Valve Lift: 0.400 inches
Inlet Valve
  Guide Length: 2.00 inches
Exhaust Valve
  Guide Length: 1.90 inches
Inlet Valve
  Stem Guide Clearance: 0.0011 inches to 0.0019 inches
Exhaust Valve
  Stem Guide Clearance: 0.0016 inches to 0.0024 inches
Valve Spring
  Free Length: 1.555 inches (Inner)
                          1.665 inches (Outer)
Valve Spring Rate: 92.5 lb/inch (Inner)
                          185.01 lb/inch (Outer)
Inlet Valve Timing: Opens 26° B.T.D.C.
                          Closes 70° A.B.D.C.
Exhaust Valve Timing: Opens 65° B.B.D.C.
                          Closes 27° A.T.D.C.

Aston Martin DBS V8 and AMV8

The Aston Martin DBS-V8 was launched in September 1969 alongside the DBS and the DB6 Mark II. The Aston Martin V8 only got into America in October 1971 but it was short-lived as the V8 engine failed to meet US requirements for the year of 1972. The Aston Martin DBS V8 had a 5340cc all-alloy four overhead camshaft unit with Bosch fuel injection and 360bhp. But by late 1971, Weber had done its research on emissions and came up with the 42 CNF downdraught carburetter. These were a power match for the older IDAs and DCOEs and were soon better than the Bosch injection. They also helped comply with USA emission regulations.

In 1972, quad headlamps were ditched in favour of a simpler two light front

Aston Martin V8

Aston Martin DBS V8 and AMV8

Series 1	V8	April 1970 to May 1972	402 cars
Series 2	V8	April 1972 to August 1973	289 cars
Series 3	V8	August 1973 to October 1978	921 cars
Series 4	V8	October 1978 to January 1986	468 cars
Series 5	V8	January 1986 to October 1989	202 cars

Financial trouble in 1974 meant that V8 production was halted for two years. The introduction of four Weber IDF downdraught carburetors was to enable the V8 to breathe better but the camshaft profiles were changed and larger valves were fitted. Power output went from 306 bhp to 360 bhp at 5800 rpm, and eventually to 406 bhp at 6200 rpm. The rear track had to be widened and different Koni dampers had to be fitted along with stiffer rear springs.

The Vantage model was introduced in 1977 and is recognizable by its blanked-off grille and bonnet scoop. The Vantage had a Stage 2 tuned engine with still larger Webers.

Aston Martin DBS V8 and AMV8

The chassis number sequences of the various models ran as follows:-

Series 1   V8   Chassis Number DBSV8/10001/R
                     to Chassis Number DBSV8/10405/R

Series 2   V8   Chassis Number V8/10501
                     to Chassis Number V8/10789

Series 3   V8   Chassis Number V8/11102   (and V8 12010)
                     to Chassis Number V8/12000   (to V8 12031)

Series 4   V8   Chassis Number V8/12032
(Oscar India)   to Chassis Number V8/12499

Series 5   V8   Chassis Number V8/12500
                     to Chassis Number V8/12701

Rear tail light of an Oscar India. Chassis Numbers were V8/12032-12499 for
Oscar India models.

Walnut and leather on the Aston Martin Oscar India's door trim is truly superb

Luxury leather seats on this Aston Martin Oscar India are well restored

Aston Martin DBS V8 and AMV8

Side view of the Aston Martin Vantage

Rear tail light of the Aston Martin Vantage, this one is registered as 256 EAD

Aston Martin DBS V8 and AMV8

The Aston Martin V8 at Woburn Abbey

The Aston Martin V8 Convertible (Volante) became a viable project when there was a gap left by the Jensen Interceptor Convertibles disappearance from production. Harold Beach styled an ageless shape.

Aston Martin V8
Colour Gallery

This car is registered AS 4087

Door trim oozes quality

Aston Martin V8
Colour Gallery

Instrumentation is surrounded by walnut

Above photograph shows control switches

Aston Martin V8 Specifications

Performance
Maximum Speeds

Gear	mph	kph	rpm
Top (mean)	146	235	5,570
Top (best)	147	237	5,600
Inter	108	174	6,000
Low	64	103	6,000

Acceleration
Gear ratios and time in seconds

mph	Top (3.07-6.14)	Inter (4.45-8.9)	Low (7.52-5.04)
0-20			1.5
10-30			1.8
20-40			2.0
30-50		2.9	2.1
40-60	4.2	3.3	2.5
50-70	4.8	3.7	
60-80	5.7	4.0	
70-90	6.4	4.4	
80-100	6.8	5.3	
90-110	7.5		
100-120	9.3		

Gearing
(with GR70VR 15in. tyres)

Top	26.2mph per 1,000rpm
Inter	18.1mph per 1,000rpm
Low	10.7mph per 1,000rpm

Brakes
Fade (from 70mph in neutral)
Pedal load for 0.5g stops in lb

1	40-35	6	40-35
2	40-37	7	40-35
3	45-35	8	45-35
4	45-35	9	50-35
5	40-35	10	50-35

Brakes
Response from 30mph in neutral

Load	g	Distance
40lb	0.37	81ft
60lb	0.75	40ft
80lb	1.04	37.6ft
100lb	1.05	28.7ft
Hand brake	0.42	72ft
Max. gradient		1 in 3

Standing ¼ mile
14.7 sec 97mph

Standing Kilometre
26.7 sec 122 mph
Test Distance
1,520 miles
Mileage Recorder
1.3 per cent under-reading

Aston Martin V8 Specifications

Acceleration

True Speed	30	40	50	60	70	80	90	100	110	120
Indicated Speed	30	40	50	60	70	80	90	100	110	120
Time in secs	2.6	3.7	4.8	6.2	8.2	10.2	12.7	15.7	19.8	25.0

Comparisons

Maximum Speed mph

Maserati Indy 4.7	(£9,677)	156mph
Porsche Carrera RS Touring	(£7,193)	149mph
Aston Martin V8	**(£9,593)**	**146mph**
Jensen SP	(£7,320)	143mph
Jaguar E-Type V12	(£3,580)	142mph

0-60mph in Seconds

Porsche Carrera RS Touring	5.5
Aston Martin V8	**6.2**
Jaguar E-Type V12	6.8
Jensen SP	6.9
Maserati Indy 4.7	7.5

Standing ¼ mile in Seconds

Porsche Carrera RS Touring	14.1
Jaguar E-Type V12	14.6
Aston Martin V8	**14.7**
Jensen SP	14.8
Maserati Indy 4.7	15.6

Overall MPG

Porsche Carrera RS Touring	16.7
Jaguar E-Type V12	15.2
Maserati Indy 4.7	13.9
Jensen SP	13.0
Aston Martin V8	**12.4**

Aston Martin V8 Specifications

Specification
(Front Engine, Rear-Wheel Drive)

Engine		Wheels	
Cylinders	8 in 90-deg vee	Type	Cast aluminium
Main Bearings	5		alloy, ventrilated
Cooling System	Water; pump,		7in. wide rim
	thermostat and	Tyres-make	Avon
	viscous-coupling fan	Tyres-type	Radial ply tubed
Bore	100mm (3.94in.)	Tyres-size	GR70VR 15in.
Stroke	85mm (3.35in.)		
Displacement	5,340cc (326 cu. in.)	**Equipment**	
Valve Gear	Twin overhead	Battery	12 Volt 68 Ah.
	camshafts per	Alternator	75 amp
	cylinder bank	Headlamps	Halogen 110/120 watt
Comp. ratio	9-to-1 Min. octane	Reversing lamp	Standard
	rating: 97RM	Electric Fuses	12
Carburettors	Four Weber	Screen Wipers	Two-speed, with
	downdraught twin-choke 42 DCNF 27		flick-wipe provision
		Screen Washer	Standard, electric
Fuel Pump	Twin SU Electric	Interior Heater	Standard, water valve
Oil Filter	Full-flow, remote		control
	mounting	Heated backlght	Standard
Max. Power	Not quoted	Safety Belts	Standard
Max. Torque	Not quoted	Interior Trim	Leather seats, nylon headlining
Transmission		Floor Covering	Wilton carpet
Gearbox	Chrysler Torque Flite	Jack	Hydraulic pillar
	3-speed epicyclic with	Jacking Points	4, under sills
	torque converter	Windscreen	Laminated
Final Drive	Hypoid bevel, limited-slip, 3.07-to-1	Underbody Protection	Bitumastic treatment after painting

Aston Martin V8 Specifications

Chassis and Body		Maintenance	
Construction	Steel box-section chassis with steel	Fuel Tank	21 Imp. gals (95 ltrs)
		Cooling System	32 pints (inc. heater)
	superstructure and aluminium body	Engine Sump	20 pints (11.3 litres) SAE 20/50. Change oil every 2,500 miles. Change filter every 5,000 miles.
Suspension			
Front	Independent, double wishbones, coil		
		Gearbox	15 pints. SAE ATF-A. Change every 20,000 miles.
	springs, telescopic dampers		
Rear	De Dion axle located	Final Drive	3.5 pints. SAE EP90LS.
	by twin radius rods each side and Watts		Change every 10,000 miles.
	linkage coils springs, level arm dampers	Grease	6 points/2,500 miles 4 points/10,000 miles
		Valve Clearnce	Inlet 0.008-0.009 in. Exhaust 0.012-0.013 in.
Steering			
Type	Adwest power assisted	Contact Breaker	0.022 in.
	rack and pinion	Ignition Timing	10 deg. BTDC (static)
Wheel dia.	15 in.		30 deg. BTDC (strobo. at 3,000 rpm)
Brakes		Spark Plug	Type: Champion N9Y.
Make and Type	Girling ventilated disc		Gap: 0.025 in.
	front and rear, divided	Compression	
	hydraulic circuits	Pressure	140-150 psi

Aston Martin Volante

February 1977 had seen an extension of the range with the introduction of the Vantage model which with its 481 DF Weber Carburetters gave it a considerable power increase.

When Aston Martin re-established its American dealerships in 1976, requests for a convertible version were being made and with the demise of the Jensen Interceptor Convertible, Harold Beach drew one towards the end of 1976, detailing the hood mechanisms. Half way through 1977 the go-ahead was given to the design and it went into production. The car was introduced to the range in June 1978. The American market took all of the 1978 production making the Aston Martin Volante a success.

Aston Martin Volante

The Aston Martin Volante featured a double-lined hood and when it was raised there was little difference from being in a saloon. Even in 1980, sales of the Aston Martin Volante were still good in the American market with them taking 39 Aston Martin Volantes that year.

Although the Aston Martin Volante was available in 1977, it was ten years before an Aston Martin Volante was available with Vantage power (the 1987 Aston Martin Vantage Volante). Aston Martin Volantes and Vantages were produced from April 1972 to October 1989 with 656 Aston Martin V8 Volante (Series 1) cars being produced and 245 Aston Martin V8 Volante (Series 2) cars being produced.

166 Aston Martin Vantage Volantes were built and another 26 Aston Martin Vantage Volantes with "power spec". Some Aston Martin Vantage Volante look-alikes were made for the US market.

Aston Martin V8
(Oscar India and current model)

Chassis series

Included in range from V8/SOR/12032 onwards. Build period (including prototypes) from August 1978 onwards. Current production

Body style(s)

Reshaped bonnet with original air-intake blanked off, as V8 'Vantage' and 'Volante'. Spoiler incorporated in boot-lid, as V8 'Vantage'. Bumper overriders. Interior modifications as detailed below

Engine, transmission and chassis

(Oscar India) As AM V8 (Stage 1) but exhaust system in stainless steel

From June 1980 (V580 engine prefix), new cylinder heads with larger valves and smaller ports, modified piston crowns and reduced valve overlap. Vacuum-controlled ignition advance. Compression ratio increased to 9.3:1. Torque converter lock-up. New dampers

Equipment

Redesigned interior similar to 'Volante' with walnut-faced facia, clock housing, glove-compartment lid and door cappings, plus new centre console. Cloth headlining replaced by leather. Carpet on lower door panels. Variable wiper delay, interior-light fade switch, new head restraints, improved air-conditioning, etc.

From June 1980, remote locking for filler flaps and boot-lid, gas-filled bonnet struts, etc.

Optional equipment at extra cost includes headlamp wash/wipe, rear foglamps, auxiliary driving lights, badge bar, electric door mirror on passenger's side, rear safety belts, lambswool rugs and seat covers, non-standard paint or trim, black leather luggage, etc. Manual transmission, £1000 extra until early 1979; thereafter available at no extra cost. Cruise control optional from June 1980

Dimensions

As quoted by manufacturers, identical to those of original fuel-injection AM V8, including kerb weight

General

Engine specification, etc., varied to suit local regulations and requirements

Aston Martin V8
(First carburettor model and Stage 1 development)

Chassis series Included in range 11002/RCA to 12031/RCAS, but excluding numbers not used, not completed, or allocated to other models. Build period (including prototypes) October 1972 to September 1978 (first Stage 1 chassis built March 1977, announced June). Production total, 977 cars

Body style(s) As AM V8 (fuel injection) but with higher and longer bulge in bonnet top. Modified air extraction at rear. Enlarged luggage compartment. Further improved insulation to engine compartment. Internal modifications as detailed below

Engine (a) Fuel injection replaced by four downdraught twin-choke 42-mm Weber carburettors. Modified valve timing. Improved engine cooling
(b) Greater valve overlap and polynomial cam profiles. Exhaust system as used on V8 'Vantage'

Transmission Improved cooling for automatic transmission. Final-drive ratios of 3.54 and 3.07:1 reintroduced

Chassis As AM V8 (fuel injection) model, but fitted with Koni dampers (as V8 'Vantage') from January 1977 and 25-Imp. Gall (114-litre) fuel tank from October 1977

Equipment Many detail changes during production life, including:
(a) Revised front seats, new switches (e.g. rocker switches replaced by 'push on, push off'), fuses grouped under glove compartment, electric lock to passenger's door, and option of 'Cosmic Fire' metallic finish
(b) From March 1977, new instruments without chrome bezels, white figures on black dials (to reduce screen reflection). Ammeter replaced by voltmeter

Dimensions As quoted by manufacturers, identical to those of fuel-injection AM V8, including kerb weight

General Engine specification, etc., varied to suit local regulations and requirements (e.g. exhaust emission control equipment and 8.3:1 compression ratio for North American market; Stage 1 engine development not applicable to US-specification cars)

Aston Martin Sanction II Zagato DB4 GTs

Of the 19 Aston Martin Zagato DB4 GTs built in the 1960 to 1963 period, four chassis numbers (0192, 0196, 0197 and 0198) were allocated but not built at that time.

They were subsequently built under the supervision of former Aston Martin factory man Richard Williams. Former Aston Martin Team manager Richard Williams believes you could not tell the older and the later built Aston Martin Zagatos.

Victor Gauntlett acknowledged that "the integrity is convincing". Only the four spare chassis numbers allocated at the time were taken up. And it was in 1987 that Victor Gauntlett and Peter Livanos decided that the cars for the four spare chassis numbers would be built. They were built in the old way with the rolling chassis being sent to Zagato in Italy for the bodies to be fabricated and fitted.

By 1989, Richard Williams had completed the rolling chassis. His own original Aston Martin DB4 GT Zagato was sent out to Italy and used as a model. Of the four cars, three had Zagato style bonnets (featuring the three-hump Zagato style) while one had a Richard Williams styled bonnet looking more Aston Martin. The Sanction II Zagatos, as the cars have come to be known, were built at Richard Williams' premises in Cobham, Surrey and have 4.2 litre engines rather

The Aston Martin DB4 Zagatos boot contained a 30 gallon petrol tank and spare wheel

than the 3.7 litre engines of the original Aston Martin DB4 Zagatos. Additionally, experience has proved that the 45DCOE4 carburettors perform better with extended inlet manifolds and therefore these have been fitted to the four DB4 GT Sanction II Zagato cars. The geometry of the front suspension was also slightly altered on the later four cars and they weighed 2515lbs as against 2550lbs of the 1960's cars.

The transmission is standard on the "new" Aston Martin DB4 GT Zagatos (0192, 0196, 0197, 0198) with Borg and Beck twin-plate clutch, David Brown close ratio four speed gearbox and 3.54 to 1 Salisbury live rear axle with a Power-Lok limited slip differential. The Sanction II cars featured the use of alternators instead of dynamos.

The back axle is braced by tubes, welded on the nose of the differential and stretching back out towards the hubs. The hubs have double wheel bearings. Road holding on the Sanction II cars should be somewhat superior to that of the original 1960s DB4 Zagatos.

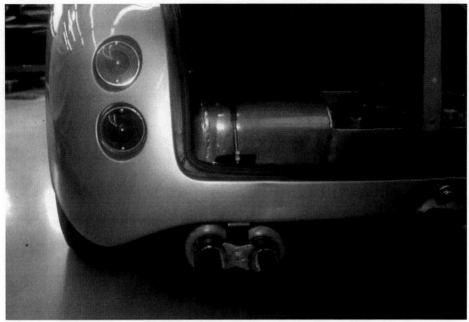

Rear light arrangement varied somewhat from car to car

Wood-trimmed steering wheel in the Aston Martin Zagato is similar to that used in Touring-bodied GTs

Engine compartment air outlet is made more attractive with the Zagato badge

The engine of the Aston Martin DB4 GT Zagato

Aston Martin Sanction II Zagato DB4 GTs

Aston Martin DB4 Zagato seen from above

The front end of the Aston Martin DB4 Zagato shows an additional air intake for the oil cooler below the radiator

Aston Martin DB4 GT Zagato

Date	Race	Drivers	Position
10-11 Jun 61	Le Mans 24 Hours (Car no. 1 in race, Chassis 0180/L)	Jean Kerguen/ Jacques Dewez/ Jean-Paul Colas	Not running at finish
10-11 Jun 61	Le Mans 24 Hours (Car no. 3 in race, Chassis 0183/R)	Lex Davison/ Bob Stilwell	Did not finish (engine)
10-11 Jun 61	Le Mans 24 Hours (Car no. 2 in race, Chassis 0182/R)	Jack Fairman/ Bernard Consten	Did not finish (engine)
19 Aug 61	Tourist Trophy (GB) (Car no. 1 in race, Reg. 1 VEV, Chassis 0182/R, completed 108 laps)	Roy Salvadori	3rd
19 Aug 61	Tourist Trophy (GB) (Car no. 3 in race, Reg. 2 VEV, Chassis 0183/R, completed 107 laps)	Jim Clark	4th
10 Sep 61	Monza Coppa Inter-Europa (Car no. 68 in race, Reg. 1 VEV, Chassis 0182/R, completed 93 laps)	Tony Maggs	2nd
10 Sep 61	Monza Coppa Inter-Europa (Car no. 62 in race, Chassis 0180/R, completed 89 laps)	Jean Kerguen	4th
22 Oct 61	Paris 1000kms (Car no. 15 in race, Chassis 0182/R, completed 126 laps)	Jim Clark/ Innes Ireland	6th
22 Oct 61	Paris 1000kms (Car no. 14 in race, completed 120 laps)	Jean Kerguen/ Jacques Dewez	14th

One Aston Martin DB4 Zagato (Chassis 0201L) was given a Bertone coupe body in 1961

Aston Martin DB4 GT Zagato

Date	Race	Drivers	Position
23-24 Jun 62	Le Mans 24 Hours (Car no. 12 in race, Chassis 0193, completed 134 laps)	Jean Kerguen/ Jacques Dewez	Did not finish (engine)
23-24 Jun 62	Le Mans 24 Hours (Car no. 14 in race, Chassis 0200, completed 124 laps)	Mike Salmon/ Ian B. Baillie	Did not finish (engine)
15-16 Jun 63	Le Mans 24 Hours (Car no. 19 in race, Chassis 0193)	Jacques Dewez/ Jean Kerguen	Did not finish (axle)
7 Jul 63	Auvergne Trophy (Car no. 1, Chassis 0193, completed 41 laps)	Jean Kerguen	18th
11 Oct 64	Paris 1000kms (Car no. 12 in race, Chassis 0183/R)	Andrew Hedges/ John Turner	Did not finish (gearbox)

Other Aston Martin Zagatos were bought and used by private owners in 1962. E. Portman ran the Aston Martin DB4 Zagato (Chassis 0117R) in the BARC. Additionally, John Coombs bought new the Aston Martin DB4 Zagato (Chassis 0190L) and drove it with Salvadori at a BRSCC meeting at Brands Hatch in May.

Aston Martin DB4 GT Zagato

Engine

Type:	6-in-line, Aluminium block and head
Bore & Stroke:	3.62 inches x 3.62 inches, 92.0 mm x 92.0 mm
Compression Ratio:	9.7 to 1
Valve Gear:	Chain-driven double overhead cams
Power:	314 bhp at 6000 rpm
Torque:	278 lb-ft at 5400 rpm

Drivetrain

Gear	Ratio	mph/ 1000 rpm	Maximum Test Speed
1st	2.49	8.5	51 mph
2nd	1.74	12.2	73 mph
3rd	1.25	17.0	102 mph
4th	1.00	21.2	127 mph

Final Drive Ratio: 3.77 to 1

Acceleration

0-30 mph	2.7 seconds
0-40 mph	3.5 seconds
0-50 mph	4.8 seconds
0-60 mph	6.0 seconds
0-70 mph	8.0 seconds
0-80 mph	9.7 seconds
0-90 mph	12.1 seconds
0-100 mph	15.0 seconds
Standing ¼ mile	15.3 seconds

Suspension

Front Suspension:	Independent unequal-length control arms, coil springs, anti roll bar, Armstrong telescopic dampers
Rear Suspension:	Rigid axle, transverse WATT linkage, 2 trailing links, coil springs, Armstrong lever arm dampers
Chassis and Body:	Full-length frame bolted and riveted to body. Hand-formed Aluminium used

Aston Martin DB4 GT Zagato

Two generations of Aston Martin Zagato

Aston Martin V8 Volante

The Aston Martin Volante included fitted leather luggage and even in automatic form could make 0-60 mph in 6.6 seconds

The switch to open or close the Aston Martin V8 Volante's roof can be seen here

Aston Martin V8 Volante

Rev-counter, oil pressure and speed instruments are set in walnut on the Aston Martin Volante

The controls for the door mirrors are seen here on this Aston Martin Volante

Aston Martin V8 Volante

A close-up picture of the glove-box shows superb quality of the material used

Cigarette lighter on the Aston Martin Volante

Aston Martin V8 Volante

The Aston Martin Volante's heating controls can be seen in this picture

Headrests on the Aston Martin Volante look slightly unusual

Steering wheel and controls of the Aston Martin V8 Volante. Walnut wood and leather everywhere

Aston Martin badge just behind the gearshift on the Aston Martin Volante

Aston Martin V8 Volante

Viva Volante!

Adverts for the Aston Martin V8 were plentiful in the 1980s

Aston Martin V8 Volante

Classic styling. Vivid performance
The 146mph Aston Martin DBS V8

See and test drive one today at
Sundridge Park Motors Ltd.
Aston Martin Distributors for Kent. Burnt Ash Lane, Bromley, Kent. Tel: 01-857 2293
Late night opening until 8.00 pm. Tuesday-Friday.   A Member of the Normand Group of Companies

Power for the few ...

Made by hand .. slowly ... to special order ...
each engine is the work of just one man ...
to provide silken power ... each interior is
hand-crafted ... a bespoke four-wheeled suit ...
a thing of beauty to enjoy forever ...
Don't just buy a car ... have an Aston Martin made.

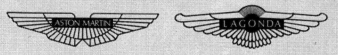

■Aston Martin (Sales) Ltd., 33 Sloane Street, London, SW1X 9NR. Tel: 01-235 8888/9. ■Aston Martin Lagonda of North America Inc., 342 West Putnam Ave., Greenwich, Conn. 06830, U.S.A. Tel: 0101-203 629 8830. ■Gillis Motors Limited, Autostrade 10, B.2660 Willebroek, Belgium. Tel: 031/86 79 71 Telex: 32644. ■Autohaus Weserspitze GmbH, Schonfelderstrasse 5-7, 3500 Kassel, West Germany. Tel: 0561 2021 (Service) 0561 23010 (Sales) Telex: 992352. ■Merz and Pabst, Parkhaus Alex, Alexanderstrasse 46, 7000 Stuttgart 1, West Germany. Tel: 0711 23 31 11 Telex: 07 21905. ■Luxhof Garage, Beckenhofstrasse 70-72, 8006 Zurich, Switzerland. Tel: 010 411 361 9777. ■Najeeb Al-Mutawa Co., P.O. Box 24801, Safat, Kuwait. Tel: 436926 Telex: 23673 Gilda K.T. ■Zubair Automotive, P.O. Box 127, Muscat, Sultanate of Oman. Tel: 722821/3 Telex: 3258 Mustrad MB. ■The International Car Centre, P.O. Box 363, Doha, Qatar. Tel: 321237 Telex: 4278. ■Saudi Arabian Markets Ltd., P.O. Box 65, Jeddah, Saudi Arabia. Tel: 688 3448/688 3548 Telex: 401067 Market SJ. ■Universal Motors, P.O. Box 246, Riyadh, Saudi Arabia. Tel: 4650591 Telex: 201271. ■Arabian Trading & Contracting Co., P.O. Box 294, Abu Dhabi, U.A.E. Tel: 971 2 334455 Telex: 22296. ■Bob Jane Southern Motors, 19 Flemington Road, North Melbourne, Australia 3051. Tel: (03) 329 9833 Telex: AA 31228. ■M.D. Motors Ltd., 2nd Floor, Elizabeth House, 250 Gloucester Road, Hong Kong. Tel: 5-7903636 Telex: HX 63481 (MDM). ■Leyland Japan Sales Limited, 1-1-11 Hatanodai, Shinagawa-Ku, Tokyo, Postal No. 142, Japan. Tel: 03 (781) 8131 Telex: 246.6638. ■House of Sports Cars (Pty) Ltd., Corner Jan Smuts and 7th Avenue, Parktown North, Johannesburg 2001, South Africa. Tel: 788 5218/9 Telex: 4-27093.

Aston Martin V8 Vantage Volante

The Aston Martin V8 Vantage Volante had the 403 bhp Vantage engine. With the manual transmission it made 0-60 mph in 5.2 seconds

The Aston Martin V8 Vantage Volante had more aggressive looking side-skirts and wheel-arches and a boot lip that curved upwards. Top speed was 160 mph